Masks

by Lola M. Schaefer

Consulting Editor:
Gail Saunders-Smith, Ph.D.

Consultant:
Terry Kuseske
National Council for
the Social Studies

Pebble Books

an imprint of Capstone Press
Mankato, Minnesota

1

Pebble Books are published by Capstone Press
818 North Willow Street, Mankato, Minnesota 56001
http://www.capstone-press.com

Library of Congress Cataloging-in-Publication Data
Schaefer, Lola M., 1950–
    Masks/by Lola M. Schaefer.
    p. cm.—(Fall fun)
    Includes bibliographical references and index.
    Summary: Describes different kinds of masks and shows how face paint can be
a part of a disguise.
    ISBN 0-7368-0106-5
    1. Masks—Juvenile literature. [1. Masks. 2. Disguise.] I. Title. II. Series: Schaefer,
Lola M. 1950– Fall fun.
GT1714.DS33   1999
391. 4'34—dc21   98-19939
                                                                                            CIP
                                                                                            AC

Note to Parents and Teachers

This series supports units on fall celebrations. This book describes
and illustrates several kinds of masks, including face paints. The
photographs support emergent readers in understanding the text.
Repetition of words and phrases helps emergent readers learn new
words. This book introduces emergent readers to vocabulary used
in this subject area. The vocabulary is defined in the Words to Know
section. Emergent readers may need assistance in reading some
words and in using the Table of Contents, Words to Know, Read
More, Internet Sites, and Index/Word List sections of the book.

Table of Contents

4

Masks hide faces.

Bunny masks hide faces.

8

Pumpkin masks hide faces.

Ghost masks hide faces.

Paint makes faces.

Stripes make tiger faces.

Whiskers make cat faces.

18

Red noses and red lips
make clown faces.

Eye patches and mustaches make pirate faces.

Words to Know

eye patch—a piece of cloth a person wears to cover an eye

ghost—a spirit of a person who has died

mask—a covering a person wears on the face

mustache—hair that grows on a person's top lip

paint—a liquid used to color something; people use special paints to color their faces.

pirate—a person who steals from ships at sea; pirates are sometimes characters in stories.

whisker—a long hair near the mouths of some animals

Read More

Beaton, Clare. *Masks.* Fun to Do. Bethany, Mo.: Fitzgerald Books, 1995.

Doney, Meryl. *Masks.* World Crafts. New York: Franklin Watts, 1995.

Long, Teddy Cameron. *Super Masks and Fun Face Painting.* New York: Sterling Publishing, 1997.

McNiven, Helen, and Peter McNiven. *Making Masks.* First Arts & Crafts. New York: Thomson Learning, 1995.

Internet Sites

Costumes
http://www.netfix.com/poptart/costume.htm

We Put on Masks
http://www.hollister.goleta.K12.ca.us/gallery/mask1.html

Index/Word List

bunny, 7
cat, 17
clown, 19
eye patches, 21
faces, 5, 7, 9, 11, 13, 15, 17, 19, 21
ghost, 11
hide, 5, 7, 9, 11
lips, 19
make, 13, 15, 17, 19, 21

masks, 5, 7, 9, 11
mustaches, 21
noses, 19
paint, 13
pirate, 21
pumpkin, 9
red, 19
stripes, 15
tiger, 15
whiskers, 17

Word Count: 41
Early-Intervention Level: 5

Editorial Credits
Martha Hillman, editor; Clay Schotzko/Icon Productions, cover designer;
    Sheri Gosewisch, photo researcher
Photo Credits
Doris Van Buskirk, 4
Photri-Microstock/Lisa Sardan, 8
Photo Network/Mark Sherman, 6
Unicorn Stock Photos/Alice M. Prescott, 1; Robin Rudd, 14; Gerry Schnieders, 16;
Wayne Floyd, 20
Valan/Phillip Norton, cover; Kennon Cooke, 10; Don Loveridge, 12
Visuals Unlimited/Richard Thom, 18